BEING RESILIENT
THE PATH TO SELF-POWERMENT

GPS to
Self-Powerment

Dr. Faye Mandell

"An eminently practical book and powerful pointer to the truth."

Eckhart Tolle, author of the #1 New York Times bestseller *The Power of Now*

GPS to Self-Powerment

Copyright © 2013 by Faye Mandell, Ph.D.

Second Edition Editors: Kathryn Middleton, April Miller, Christian Pacheco, Donna Melillo
Second Edition Cover Design: Levatas / www.levatas.com
Second Edition Interior Design: Rick Soldin / book-comp.com

Printed in the United States of America

Library of Congress Control Number: 2013958054

ISBN: 978-0-9860493-7-8

Second Edition

being-present.com

GPS to
Self-Powerment

Dr. Faye Mandell

To those who are bold enough to consider
new possibilities

Contents

Condensed Preface

Although this is a second edition, there have been countless revisions to this book. I have included a condensed version of the preface from the first edition, written by my original publisher, because she writes so beautifully and says such very wise things:

This book is truly a Life Book—a book for everyone in human form today—but within that universal application, we focus on showing how this model can be specifically applied to the business sector. This is done by means of certain dialogues, examples, and one chapter that is devoted to this audience. We could have, indeed, added other chapters applying this model to other life areas: conflict resolution, parenting, and creative problem solving, to name only a few. However, we chose to keep this book short with the belief that more people will then read it and thereby be reached by it.

Most books lend themselves to a particular genre. For them, it is relatively easy to establish a clear organizing principle and achieve an overall vital cohesiveness. Since Self-Powerment proposes a new way of looking at how we think and communicate, it calls for its own unique structure. It attests to the statement, "You can't put new wine in old bottles." Not only did we need a new kind of container for this book, but we also needed to coin words that express the new perceptions and new understandings.

From the beginning of the book until the end, we hear Faye's unique voice guide us as if we were in one of her workshops. She conveys her message sincerely and in practical language.

My work as a publisher provides a special gift: the opportunity to work closely and soulfully with authors during the prepublication process and to become authentic friends thereafter. With Faye Mandell, I encountered a commitment to her work that is singular. Atypical in a publisher-author relationship, it was she who wanted to hurry, hurry this book to press. Faye comes from the maelstrom-like energy of the eastern seaboard in the United States, and I now know what it means when someone wants something done "in a New York minute." So, I am happy to finally release this book, even if, much to the frustration of its author, it took its own time to come into being.

—Connie Kellough,
President, Namaste Publishing Inc.

A Modern Parable

Once upon this current time, there is man named Every Person, EP for short, who lives a limited life—a life predominantly of striving, worrying, and never feeling he's good enough or achieving enough. Most of the time, EP lives in his head, dealing with his day by fretting about the future, having regrets about the past, and fantasizing about what could be. Every once in a while, however, EP experiences the security, the creativity, and the completeness that make him feel truly wonderful. Then, he says, "Now, this is how we are supposed to live!" It is as if he hears a familiar bell signaling to him that he has arrived home.

These occasions are rare, however. One day, after a rare and most enjoyable moment, he suddenly finds himself back at the office with his heavy "To Do" file, worrying about twenty things. "How do I get from the Here-Now to the office today?" he asks himself. "What happened? Why couldn't I just continue to enjoy this moment and stay in the present without the thoughts that pulled me away?"

These sincerely posed questions set him on a course of exploration and self-observation. He notes that it is his own thinking that takes him out of his present contentment and into other times and places.

Continuing with this self-observation, he discovers how certain feelings and thoughts work together. He notes that it is when he feels fear, anger, and guilt that he starts thinking in a way that takes him on disturbing and useless journeys away from the Here-Now. He follows this back further and finds that it is when he isn't feeling secure, in control, and adequate that he starts thinking this way. He experiments with just staying with his feelings and not allowing them to take him into thought.

Then, an amazing thing happens. As EP continues in this awareness and practice, he finds that he starts to experience more and more moments in which he just enjoyed being with himself with no thought. This is so new of an experience for him that he finds it hard to describe it to others. The joy and ensuing benefits of this experience lead EP to go intentionally back to the Here-Now many times a day; he especially knows to go there if something or someone threatens his inner equilibrium in ways that bring up his need to remain secure, in control, and adequate. The more often he goes back to this inner place, the more he finds his life changes in wonderful ways: He finds that he comes up with creative ideas and solutions to the challenges of life as he meets them. He finds that he has more energy and is able to focus on what is truly important in life. He finds that he worries less and less and enjoys each moment more and more. His family, too, recognizes how much more at ease he is and how he seems to really enjoy being with them fully.

EP realizes he has made a great discovery. He feels like he has removed a central brick from a wall; and with that one brick's removal, he has brought down a whole limiting structure so that he can now see beyond to a new reality.

EP marvels at how his life has changed so suddenly and how he is able to toss away his worries, his feelings of inadequacy, and his artificial needs so easily. It's as if he has moved to a different territory and, because of that, experiences life differently. "How did I get from my former way of life to Here-Now?" he asks sincerely.

"Ah," says his muse, "this is what the book in your hand is all about."

Introduction

"It's ridiculous!" That's what most of the people I work with hear me saying over and over. It's ridiculous to worry about the future and not act to make it happen. I have never created a future scenario in my head that actually happened.

It's ridiculous to spend time and energy regretting the past. You can't change it! Use the time and energy to learn and be wiser. It's ridiculous to focus on other people and to judge, compare, and negate them when everything you need in this world is already inside yourself. Reality is created by where you put your attention. What you attend to is what is created in your experience. You were taught by your parents, teachers, friends, and family what was important to them, which now has become what you **think** is important. I emphasize the word "think" because we have no idea how much time and energy we spend creating thoughts. Thought takes us out of the present and into other places in time and space: future, past, other people. By using images and language, thought wants to know about stuff because thought is always about stuff. Since we put attention on our thoughts, we are always thinking about stuff rather than experiencing our lives. That's what is so ridiculous.

When we can get the information we want from experience, why do we value thinking about the stuff? *Yet that is what we do: we think about the future.* Here's a scenario: You have a client who cancels an appointment. You think, "I will never hear from them again. I will lose the account. I will get fired, and I will be a bag lady in New York City." Honestly, this is where most people find themselves. Now, imagine a bag lady in New York City. When you create these thoughts and put your attention on them, they become real, and where you REALLY are is LOST—*really* lost. You are no longer seeing, hearing, tasting, and touching what is actually happening. Really!

I used to believe that time and space concepts only belonged in the realm of physics. I had no idea that how people experience time and space is the GPS to getting to and staying in the present moment, and this is how it happened.

It's amazing that I was able to get through my whole educational experience without having taken a physics course.

In my naiveté at that time, I just thought that physics was something to be feared. Physics was for smart, scientific people, not for real people. Imagine four years of college, a master's, and a doctorate without one physics course. After finishing my last degree, I went to work. One night, I was browsing through an adult education brochure and saw a description of a course called "Quantum Physics and the Face of God." I just knew that I had to take it. I dragged two of my colleagues along; and from that day forward, my life has never been the same. Although part of the course dealt with mathematical formulas, most of it dealt with the relationship of physics to awareness. I was surprised that there was a connection between physics and psychology. It was as if a vast door unlocked, making a primal connection for me. I was hooked.

Furthermore, I had no idea that I was engaging in transformational possibilities. I didn't even know what transformational possibilities meant. I was a psychologist and was interested in helping people. I never before understood that there was another whole level, or more, of awareness that until now had been unavailable to me.

The relationship between physics and awareness became my focus, allowing me to shift my view of reality. We are taught certain things in our culture about what exists and what does not. Our thoughts are regarded as truth in our society, and it never dawned on me to question the validity of my thoughts.

However, before I could detach from my own thoughts, I spent most of my time doing just that— believing and listening to the racket of thoughts that would control my attention at all times of the day. For instance, when out with other people, I spent energy constantly comparing myself to them and finding myself inferior. Whether at work, at a party, or just in a public setting, much of my energy and focus was on my nagging insecurities or on what others might have (looks, money, talent, and so forth) that I did not.

I gave time and energy to my thoughts that created these insecurities. When I looked in the mirror, I always saw the things that were wrong with me. I had a habit of creating scenarios in my head of what I should have done to look prettier or say something smarter. By doing this, I was living in the past and feeling guilty, and I focused on others, feeling angry. The relationship between where you are internally and what you are feeling is a fundamental component of this book. You will read about this concept throughout the book. It is a new awareness that results from the relationship of time and space to feeling states.

Because I focused my attention and energy on those totally unproductive thoughts of guilt and anger, I believed they were facts. By spending my time on these thoughts, I was fulfilling my own prophecy.

At that point, it never occurred to me that there were alternative ways to understand my relationship to others and myself. Teachers, friends, or other sage folk may have *tried* to show me this, but they made little progress because I trusted my thoughts. Along with the high value we place on thoughts, there is also a devaluation of feelings.

By going along with society's general negation of feelings, I tried to fit in, but I never felt at ease. There was a constant battle within me between what I was told was right and appropriate and what I felt. I couldn't speak of these conflicting experiences because I didn't have the words or concepts yet to do this; but I did know that I did not feel clear, focused, or at peace. As a matter of fact, I felt disease (dis-ease), and this continued throughout my life until I bumped directly into the interrelationship between psychology and physics.

Then, with my new discoveries, I began to understand the uneasiness I had felt all my life. I began to see beyond my own limited perspective. There was a dimly lit recognition that I had touched upon something magical—something unknown—a virtual gateway to possibilities. I became aware that when you experience life directly in the present moment and use thoughts in a more limited manner, you open to a whole new way of being.

My gut feeling of what life is all about was affirmed. The "shoulds," the "what-ifs," and the thoughts about needing to be perfect, lovable, attractive, and smart were just that—only thoughts. These are thoughts that compare, judge, and negate.

I have discovered that thoughts by themselves are different from the actual experience of living. Instead of clarifying and being helpful in practical ways, I realized that thoughts, being at least one step away from the direct experience of the present moment, can also distort, confuse, and mislead. I became aware that the fleeting glimpses of clarity, focus, ease, and gratitude I felt when experiencing life directly in the Here-Now could be expanded so that I could spend more of my life appreciating the present rather than judging, comparing, negating, worrying, being angry, or feeling guilty for who I am.

These discoveries were so new and so thrilling that I felt both excitement and apprehension. Through reading, I began to explore more about this gateway of using the hard sciences, such as physics, to explore awareness. Reading from a lay perspective in physics and having, through years of schooling, a highly intellectual perspective in psychology, I felt a unique awareness of how these two disciplines could be interwoven. Over time, this awareness has led to the development of a working empirical model which relies on the interconnectedness of the two disciplines to make practical, everyday use of both of them: the Self-Powerment Model.

The model that is being presented in this book combines elements from the disciplines of psychology and physics. Because of the interdisciplinary nature of this model, and because I am presenting new material, common terms such as "thought," "feeling," "time," and "space," among other concepts, are redefined and used in novel ways to convey the new understandings—the new awareness.

Language has always had to adjust to accommodate our growing consciousness and changing worldview. In this book, you encounter new terms, such as "wobble," "piggyback," "feeling-thought," "Here-Now," and "self-powerment."

I define these terms in the new context I am using them in. For your reference, there is a glossary at the back of the book as well. These new words and definitions might feel a bit unusual and alien until you become familiar with them. Try to remain open to the way they are being used in the model. When new material is presented, we have a habit of going into judgment, comparison, and negation to avoid experiencing it. Often, we try to guard and protect our current perception of the way we believe things are. It is fundamental to remember that as long as we are judging, we cannot fully experience changes in awareness. Because of this, I request that for the duration of your reading of this book, you suspend any impulse you might have to compare the Self-Powerment Model to other workshops you have attended or material that you have read and refrain from premature conclusions. New ideas need to live long enough to have a chance to prove their validity and worth. Watch your thought process in action. Negative thoughts, such as "This won't work for me," "I've already tried this," or "It can't be that simple," are killer thoughts. These always have a negative message that ultimately does not allow us to see clearly. Watch for these and become an aware observer of your thoughts. As I have said, see them for what they are—just thoughts. You exist apart from them.

As Eckhart Tolle said in *The Power of Now*, "The single most vital step on your journey toward enlightenment is this: learn to disidentify from your mind."[1] This is a valuable instruction, and the Self-Powerment Model provides a practical, step-by-step way in which to do this in our daily lives.

When you read, don't hurry to the conclusion. When a new term is being used or an important concept is being explained, it is a good idea to pause and let yourself experience it. In this book, I share with you things you already know but have been covered up by learned ways of thinking. When you experience a moment directly, you are returning to information that has always been within you but has been put into such artificial categories that it is no longer accessible.

For example, many children are placed in the category of "slow learners," yet these children are gifted in so many ways. As soon as we have separated them into a category, we are unlikely to see them in their true capacity—in their fullness. The Self-Powerment Model provides a way to bypass these artificial categories and return to direct experience in the Here-Now. Many people have written about the benefits of living in the Here-Now. **In this book, I provide a practical, simple way to get and live there.**

Communicating
Some New Ideas

As a student of psychology, I found two major topics that aroused my interest: feelings and thoughts. I will discuss both of these terms in this chapter. It is important that you be introduced to the way we use them in the Self-Powerment Model before moving on to the model itself. Other terms that will be discussed are time and space, Here-Now, I Am, and feeling-thoughts.

When I became more skilled at listening to people differently, I observed that although the content of what people said varied, whenever they spoke about their worries and fears, they were always talking about the future. Whenever they talked about their regrets and guilt, they were always talking about the past. Whenever they talked about their anger, they were always focused on other people and things outside themselves or on a very narrow aspect of themselves. The common denominator, regardless of the specific content they were talking about, was that they were speaking from a *specific time and space perspective*, and the focus was away from their direct experience of the present moment—in other words, away from the Here-Now.

I began to realize that there was something about what we label "unpleasant" feelings that made people talk about them in any way but from a Here-Now perspective. After I started to read enthusiastically and extensively in the area of physics, I experimented with how concepts like time and space can be applied to how people talk about feelings. The culture has created its own definition of feelings. In it, feelings are devalued and seen as negative and toxic. The definition of feelings used in this book is entirely different. In the Self-Powerment Model, feelings are bodily indicators that signal a person to perform an action. For example, anxiety is a feeling that lets people know that they are losing their focus and need to direct their attention back to the present moment. That is why "feelings can serve as barometers of life management," as quoted from Antonio Demasio in his book *Self Comes to Mind*.[2] We will talk more about this further on in the chapter.

Finally, I worked on developing a model that people could use which combines some of these concepts to develop awareness. The next section presents our working definitions of these terms as they are used in the Self-Powerment Model.

Thought

Thinking is a capacity that develops over time. Though initially it was used for certain purposes, we have learned over time to think about everything. We all have used phrases like, "Let's think about it," "Think before you speak," "We need to give it more thought," and "Let's try to think outside the box." The act of thinking is highly esteemed in our society. Despite this, most of us think without giving much attention to the actual thought process. The dictionary definition of thought is simply "the product of mental activity." Most of us do not realize how much power our thoughts have over us. When we begin to grasp this, we can begin to shift that power so that we can use thought for our own self-powerment.

A key to self-powerment is to observe thoughts in an objective way. It is to our advantage to become the outside observer of our thoughts. In the Self-Powerment Model, different aspects of thought are introduced. We explore how we create our thoughts—that is, we look at the structure of a thought.

The structure of thought has two dimensions: time and space. The structure of thought tells us (1) where we are in time (that is, past, present, future) and (2) where we are in space (that is, where our attention is focused).

For example, when we go to a movie, as soon as the movie is over, we think and talk about that experience. We likely talk about just a few aspects of the movie— specific fragments that caught our attention or piqued our interest such as the plot line, a certain character, or the special effects.

We call the actual experience of watching the movie **direct experience**. We call the things we talk about **the content of our thoughts**. We call where this content takes us in time and space **the structure of the thought**. In the Self-Powerment Model, the structure of the thought is where the thought takes us in time and space. When a thought occurs, being conscious of where we are in time (past, present, future) and where we are in space (where our attention is focused) is a new experience for most of us. Observing this gives us a new way to detach from the content of our thoughts. Really, we no longer need to focus on the content of our thoughts. We have another choice. With the Self-Powerment Model, we can focus on where that thought takes us in time and space. We have never been told that having an awareness of where we are in time and space is so important and that focusing on a different aspect of thought (its structure) can shift our attention from the content of a thought. That's what is so exciting!

Time and Space

The Self-Powerment Model's working definition of **time** places us in the past, present, or the future. Our working definition of **space** lets us know where our attention is focused. In everyday terms, time and space are perceived as separate. Time is seen as a limited interval or period, and space is seen as an expanse in which material objects are located. Actually, time and space are important because they are points of reference for us. They define and shape an experience. For example, "The project will take three weeks," or "Yesterday was my father's birthday." Time and space limit and define experience. They are important concepts because they help us locate and reference direct experience and communicate the experience to others.

In this book, time and space take on a whole new value: they help us to locate ourselves when we are not in the Here-Now. In the Self-Powerment Model, time and space are seen as a continuum. In other words, time and space are experienced as one. They provide a compass for navigating to our place of Self-Powerment. Steven Johnson in his book, *Where Good Ideas Come From: The Natural History of Innovation* says, "Evolutionary biologists have a word for this kind of borrowing: exaptation. An organism develops a trait optimized for a specific use, but then the trait gets hijacked for a completely different function."[3]

So it is with time and space, which is used by physicists to experience the relationship of one object to another. We are using it here to act as a compass to the present moment. Using the words that make up a sentence or thought rather than focusing our attention on the ideas created by the sentence, we discover the way back to the present moment.

Thought takes us out of the present moment. As a society, we have learned to think about everything. When doing this, we leave the Here-Now without consciously choosing to do so. When we shift our attention to where these thoughts take us in time and space, we can begin to make a more conscious choice about when we want to think and when we want to have a direct experience.

Here-Now and I Am

Being in the present moment, without thought, is being in the Here-Now. The Here-Now is where we access direct experience. It is where we experience consciousness without thought. Another way to define Here-Now is I Am. To be in the I Am is to be fully in the present moment with attention focused on our internal multi-sensory experience. These two terms, "Here-Now" and "I Am," go hand in hand. As you can see, Here-Now and I Am reference time and space. It is the way we associate ourselves with time and space.

Space	Time
Here	Now
I	Am

The columns above show how we can make practical use of the concepts of space and time to position ourselves in the Here-Now, which is expressed in our language by the words "I Am."

To be in the I Am is the most wondrous state because it is in the I Am that we experience our authentic self. It is the only place where we know *what is so*. Fear, anger, and guilt no longer create our reality. We are not subjected to or limited by concepts that are created by thought. Thoughts create the structures whereby we judge, evaluate, compare, and negate and leave the Here-Now. In the I Am, we are free to experience the Here-Now in its fullness. In the I Am, all the shapes, textures, and nuances of life operate perfectly. We are fully present, aware, and at peace. We are free to create from infinite possibilities. In the I Am, the wisdom housed in our very cells is available to us. We can experience without the encumbrance of the artificial boundaries that thought imposes. We have access to the vast array of sensory information that is not limited by thought. There are so many gifts we have when we are fully in the Here-Now.

I am not the first person to know that the Here-Now—the I Am—is the place where people are self-powered. We see the I Am when Tiger Woods plays golf, Michael Jordan plays basketball, Mark McGwire plays baseball, or Venus and Serena Williams play tennis. We experience it when our child is hurt and we go into the immediate right action, or when we call a parent or relative spontaneously because we just know something is wrong. We call it "the zone." When we are in the zone, we access data from direct experience with an expanded sensory database.

In the zone, we are able to intuit our experience totally. We are self-powered. We are aware of the extraordinary amount and variation of information accessible from our senses.

Once, after taking attendance when teaching a course to college freshmen, I asked, "Who is really present? I mean whose attention is focused in this room at this time, as opposed to being somewhere else in time and space: for example, reliving a fight you had with your boyfriend last night, worrying about an assignment that is due tomorrow, or trying to figure out how you are ever going to pay back your loan for college tuition and such?" I reminded them that since I was a guest lecturer, their response would not affect their grades. Out of the forty-five students, not one could truly admit that their focus was on being in the class at that moment.

Feelings

Feelings play a vital role in our life. A feeling is a physical sensation. It is experienced in the Here-Now and has no thought component. Feelings are nature's indicators that signal to us that we need to get back to homeostasis.

Feelings let us know that our emotional needs must be tended to. Feelings are the fundamental tools that nature gives us for staying in the Here-Now, allowing us to stay in balance. In the Self-Powerment Model, we focus on three of these feelings: anxiety, frustration, and sadness. For example, when we have a half-completed report due at three o'clock, and it's already two o'clock, we experience a feeling—anxiety—that can allow us to focus and stay present with the task at hand to complete it and feel secure that we are doing our job competently. When we experience sadness at the end of an emotional relationship, the feeling allows us to know it is over and let us take accountability for our part in the ending of the relationship.

Feelings emerge in response to internal and external experiences such as missing the bus, having a flight cancelled, getting a divorce, or receiving a demotion. These experiences evoke bodily signals that are experienced as feelings. We learn to ignore these feelings because they are not valued and often not acceptable in our society. We demean natural feelings and avoid experiencing them.

Everyone knows the cliché "Men don't cry." Generally, feelings are not experienced in our society. However, feelings are the fundamental tool that nature gives us for staying in the Here-Now—for staying self-powered. Feelings are physical sensations that are experienced in the Here-Now. Natural feelings maintain balance, clarity, focus, control, and self-confidence.

Feeling-Thoughts

As seen in the previous section, we often do not allow ourselves to experience feelings. However, feelings occur all the time. Because we are not allowed to experience many of them, we have had to find a way to discharge them. We have learned to create a thought as the vehicle to do that.

Let me say this again: Since we are not able to utilize our feelings to execute actions that keep us in balance, we have learned to create a thought (the feeling creates the thought) as the way to discharge the feeling. We see them as partners in crime. We combine feelings and thoughts; and by doing this, we create a feeling-thought.

A feeling-thought is defined as a feeling that has been so inextricably bound up with thought that the pure experience of the feeling can no longer be distinguished from the thought. Compare it to making batter by mixing milk with eggs: soon, you are no longer able to see the milk separate from the egg. After a feeling has been combined with a thought, it is no longer possible to experience the feeling as separate.

We do not often allow ourselves to experience the sadness at the end of a relationship. Instead, we might focus on the "should haves," "could haves," and "would haves." When we do this, we are no longer able to distinguish the thoughts from the feelings. For instance, when we point out, "That's his house," to identify the exact location of a residence, we experience "his house" as the stage for our personal drama if we are internally thinking, "That's the house where five years ago he told me he wanted a divorce." In this way, we experience the divorce over and over again, attaching the feeling of sadness to the event. (How we use feelings naturally is explained in the chapter on the Self-Powerment Model.)

So how can we know the difference between thought and feeling? Remember that the experience of a feeling is a physical sensation with no thought component. Initially, sadness was a natural feeling without a thought. In a nanosecond, we discharged the sadness by creating thoughts. The result is thoughts of "should have," "could have," and "would have." By listening to the structure of the thoughts—that is where thoughts take us in time and space—we can reference ourselves in time and space and reconnect to the natural feeling—for example, the feeling of sadness rather than the thoughts of "should have," "could have," or "would have." It is a remarkable awakening to experience consciousness without thought. This is possible when we learn to distinguish between thought and feeling.

A feeling creates a thought, which takes us out of the Here-Now without choice. The actual content of the thought is irrelevant. The purpose of the thought is to discharge those feelings that we do not allow ourselves to experience.

Possibly as a way to identify ourselves as uniquely human or to separate ourselves from lower species, we have come to discount the importance of feelings and to exalt thought. We must remember that feelings are very real and very important.

The Self-Powerment Model allows us to remember what we already know but have not been encouraged to experience. When we don't fully experience our feelings, we can't execute the actions that keep us balanced. When we reconnect to the place where we are fully immersed in experiencing our natural feelings, we are able to open to service, compassion, integrity, accountability, and courage. We experience the fullness of life and naturally express our gratitude for the ongoing gift of it.

Time and space are universal reference points, which are indispensable to civilized society. They have tremendous practical value. They help us function on a daily basis, e.g., scheduling and attending medical appointments, work meetings, and dinner engagements. They are necessary for the mechanical processes of life such as preparing a menu or building a house. They help us to establish ownership: *my* car, *your* book, or *his* problem. In addition, they create the forum in which we do long-term planning. For example, I will get my degree in three years from my university.

However, over the thousands of years of human conditioning, we have come to expand the use of time and space. They serve to structure our thoughts, which often become the vehicles to discharge personal feelings by reverting to the past, speculating on the future, or focusing outside ourselves and away from the present moment.

By using nouns, pronouns, and verbs—the time and space words in our language—and linking them to the discharge of feelings, we personalize time and space. Time and space become meshed with feelings and the content of the thought. When we combine time, space, and feelings, the content of the thought is used only to discharge feelings. We lose the practical benefits of thought and also the choice to stay in the Here-Now.

The next chapter presents the Self-Powerment Model. This Model allows us to create a mental picture of where we are in time and space. Are we in the past, in the present, or in the future? Are we focusing on other people and things? Are we looking only at a fragment of ourselves? This internal picture becomes the means to connect to and experience our natural feelings, which when acted upon, create the space of self-powerment. Just asking ourselves, "Where am I? Who or what else is with me? Am I seeing only a fragment of myself? Am I only listening to thoughts that dwell on the past and future?" bring a new way to identify if we are in the I Am. This simple inquiry is very powerful. When we pay attention to the structure or the parts of a thought, we can choose to observe where that thought takes us in time and space. Once we have this awareness, we can choose to eliminate the thoughts that cause dis-ease and deplete our energy.

The Self-Powerment Model

It's All About Choice

In the last chapter, we established that we create thought to discharge the feelings we avoid experiencing. When we can free ourselves from those thoughts and return to direct experience, we open infinite possibilities and can exercise our free choice regarding how we want to participate in our lives.

Before I introduce the Self-Powerment Model, try this exercise: Think about eating a piece of chocolate. Describe that experience. Write it down on a piece of paper. Then, eat a piece of chocolate and write down that experience. Note the vastly different information that is accessed when you think about something versus when you experience it directly.

Thinking about your dream vacation is very different from experiencing it. When you actually take the vacation, the experience may be even better than you anticipated, or you may be disappointed. But at least through experience, you find out the truth.

The Self-Powerment Model presented here allows you the ability to choose a direct experience.

We all have biological needs. We also have indicators that let us know these needs exist. When we are hungry, our stomach growls and we get stomach pains. If we didn't listen to this indicator, we would die. When we are thirsty, we lick our lips and our mouth gets dry, so we get something to drink. When we are sleepy, our eyelids droop and we yawn. Then, we lie down and go to sleep.

Just as we have biological needs, we also have emotional needs. These needs are to be secure, be in control, and feel adequate. When these are being met, we are in the Here-Now—the I Am. I represent these needs on the time and space graph shown on the facing page.

Time-Space

In the last chapter, I introduced time and space, the building blocks for the Self-Powerment Model. The horizontal line represents time, and the vertical line represents space. It is at the intersection where the time and space lines meet that we feel secure, in control, and adequate. We represent this in our language by the words "I Am." "Am" is a present tense verb that lets us know we are in the present, and "I" is a pronoun

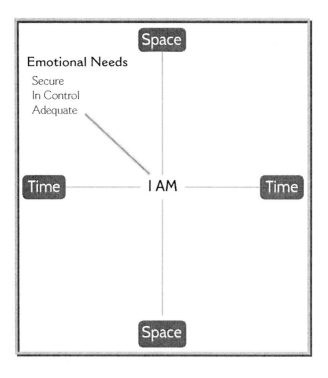

that lets us know that our attention is focused on our multisensory data.

The following are some graphs to help you observe when you leave the Here-Now. They create an internal map to assist you in observing how the structure of your thoughts can take you out of the I Am. This internal treasure map can guide you back to accessing the direct experience.

Future

When we go out on the line for time to the right, we go to the future. Some of the words that let us know we are in the future are "will," "could," "should," "might," and "what if."

Examples:

"I will never get it done."

"What if my husband loses his job?"

Take a moment to consider how often you use the words "will," "could," "should," "might," and "what if."

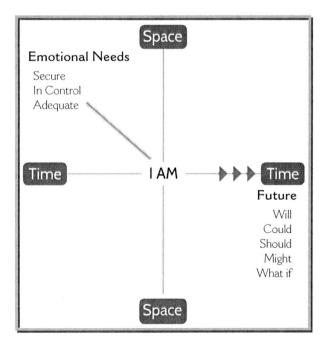

Past

When we go on the time line to the left, we go to the past. Some of the words that let us know we are in the past are "did," "had," "was," "could have," "would have," and "should have."

Examples:

"If I would have gone to college, I could have gotten a better job."

"If I could have taken the trip, I might have met the man of my dreams."

Take a moment to consider how often you use those words.

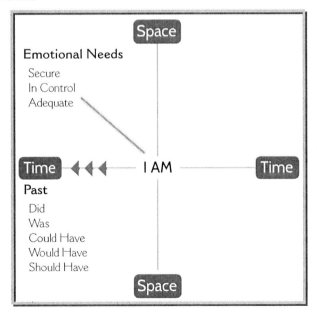

Create Others and Things

When we go up on the space line, we create other people, situations, and experiences. Some of the words that let us know we are creating other people are "he," "she," "they," and "you." Some of the words that let us know we are focusing on other things are "the budget," "the deadline," "the grades," and so forth.

Examples:

"You're being mean."

"The deadline is unrealistic."

"He is causing this disaster."

Take a moment to consider how often you use these words.

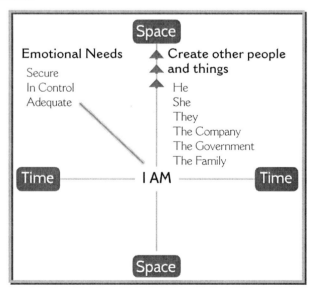

Distort

When we go down the space line, we take a fragment of our self-image and magnify it to become our whole identity: "I'm not smart enough," "I'm not strong enough," and "I'm too old."

Observe that going up or down the space line is, in both instances, merely focusing away from internal multisensory data and getting away from what is experienced internally.

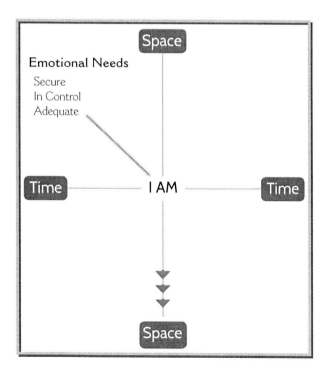

Feelings in the Self-Powerment Model

In the Self-Powerment Model, when a feeling indicates that an emotional state must be tended to, we say that state is "in wobble." These feelings translate into actions that allow us to stay secure, remain in control, and feel adequate. These actions keep us in homeostasis and in balance as well as connected to the larger experience of being one with the universe.

Just as we have indicators that let us know our biological needs are in wobble, we also have indicators that let us know our emotional needs are in wobble. These indicators are called feelings. As I have said before, nature gives us feelings for a reason. Inherent in the experience of a feeling is the action we need to take in order to feel secure, in control, and adequate—an action that enables us to stay self-powered in the Here-Now.

As mentioned earlier, a feeling is a physiological sensation that has no thought component. We can liken it to our stomach growling or our mouth getting dry. It is a biological indicator that signals us to do something to stay in the Here-Now.

In the Self-Powerment Model:

➜ The feeling that lets us know our security need is in wobble is anxiety.

→ The feeling that lets us know our control need is in wobble is frustration.

→ The feeling that lets us know our adequacy need is in wobble is sadness.

A natural feeling occurs in the present moment. When we focus our attention on it, it is a storehouse of essential information that is felt and processed simultaneously. It is our most immediate and authentic response. Each of the three natural feelings that the Self-Powerment Model addresses provide the energy that signals that we must interact with our environment in some way to stay self-powered.

Let's Look At How These Feelings Work

When we are focused inside ourselves, we rely on our own intuition, which is accessed in the Here-Now. To do this and to maintain the emotional states of security, control, and adequacy, we must experience our feelings. In order to regain this ability, we have to look at how our feelings have become negatively valued and therefore not tended to. To do this, we need to go to our early childhood to see how this happened.

First, let's look at anxiety. A little girl comes home from school and says, "Mommy and Daddy, I'm so worried about a test I have tomorrow. It's one third of my grade, and I really want to do well. I'm so nervous." Like all parents, Mommy and Daddy have learned that they do not want their daughter to be anxious. They might say, "Don't worry, honey. We'll help you study and do a good job. Please don't be anxious." The feeling is avoided by an immediate solution provided by the parents.

Let's now turn to frustration. Johnny comes home from a baseball game his team has lost and says to his parents, "I'm so frustrated. Our baseball team lost every game this season. I guess we don't practice enough. I'm just so frustrated." His parents might say, "Don't be frustrated. We'll help you practice after school and talk to the coach about practicing more often." Again, there is the strong negation of the experience of the feeling—in this case, frustration.

Finally, let's look at sadness. Sally comes home and says, "Mary's having a party. She's invited all the other girls, but not me. I'm so sad." The parents take away Sally's feeling of sadness immediately: They say, "Don't be sad. We'll make a bigger party with balloons and clowns, and we won't invite Mary."

After years of repeated reinforcement that feelings are not acceptable, we have learned not to pay attention to them. Like the children in the above examples, we have learned to not experience our feelings and use them to act on our environment to get back to balance.

Feelings cannot be eliminated, so the problem is that once a feeling is evoked, it must be discharged. Let's take a look at how this works.

Feeling-Thought: Fear

If a feeling can't be discharged by experiencing it, the feeling moves from the body to create a thought. The feeling is piggybacked onto the thought and gets discharged that way. In the Self-Powerment Model, to piggyback is to take a feeling and move it from the body onto a created thought. The act of moving a feeling, which belongs in the body, to a thought takes us out of the Here-Now—out of our place of Self-Powerment. As we know, a feeling-thought is the combination that results when a feeling gets connected to a created thought in a nanosecond—that is, it is piggybacked onto a thought.

Remember, when a feeling creates a thought, the result is that we must structure the thought in a particular way. That means that the thought must take a particular form.

We can all see how common feeling-thoughts are in our daily lives. For example, Tom has a project due at 3:00 P.M. Because there is still a lot to do, he begins to feel anxiety. That anxiety, when used naturally, allows him to stay focused, clear, and in touch with his creativity and wisdom. However, he has learned to take that anxiety and, in a nanosecond, piggyback it onto a thought, which takes him into the future. For example, he may think, "I'll never get this job done in time. They won't ever give me another opportunity to prove my capability." Now, we have this new combination of a feeling-thought. The feeling-thought of anxiety is fear or worry.

We can see this in all sorts of situations. For instance, when Rachel's boyfriend says he will be at her house at 8:00 P.M., Rachel prepares for his arrival. Time passes, and he is late. At 10 P.M., he still hasn't arrived. Carried away by her thoughts, Rachel has already decided that he is with another woman and is coming back only to tell her he is leaving her forever. This is another scenario in which the feeling of anxiety becomes the feeling-thought of fear.

Anxiety is what allows us to keep our attention on what is experienced in the moment. This focus allows us to do what is necessary to stay secure. When we find ourselves forced into the future, we have piggybacked the feeling of anxiety onto a thought we have created. When we piggyback the feeling, we create thoughts meshed with anxiety, and they are experienced as thoughts in the future. We know we are in the future when we use words like "will," "never," "what if," "always," "might," and so forth.

Emotional Needs →	Natural Feelings →	Feelings = Thoughts
Secure	anxiety	fear
In Control	frustration	anger
Adequate	sadness	guilt

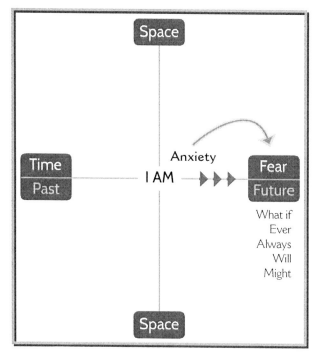

Most, if not all, of the energy needed to get the task done is used, instead, to move the feeling of anxiety and create thoughts about the future. These thoughts remove us from the present, where we are able to use the anxiety to focus and to access the creative resources we need to deal with the experience in the present. At this point, a feeling-thought created to discharge a feeling is indistinguishable from a thought that is created to imagine possibilities. We therefore have to be deliberate in our ability to focus on where we are in time and space to ensure that our thoughts are created for real reasons—for example, thoughts that innovate, create more possibilities, and bring us closer to partnering with nature to create additional abundance.

Feeling-Thought: Anger

In the following scenario, one of Shirley's children, Karen, spills some of her red finger paint onto a white carpet. As a result, Shirley feels frustrated and out of control. Rather than find the carpet cleaner or call the carpet cleaning company, Shirley begins to yell at Karen and blame her for her carelessness. Instead of experiencing the frustration, which would immediately lead to cleaning the carpet, Shirley piggybacks that frustration onto a thought, shifts the focus to her daughter, and blames Karen.

In another example, Bob places an urgent call and reaches an answering machine. Instead of using his frustration to stay in control and do something available to him, such as returning e-mails or using his energy to do productive work, while waiting to speak with the person, his frustration gets piggybacked and is experienced as thoughts: "What a jerk that guy is! Why isn't

Emotional Needs →	Natural Feelings →	Feelings = Thoughts
Secure	anxiety	fear
In Control	frustration	anger
Adequate	sadness	guilt

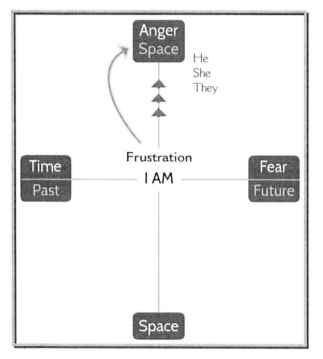

he ever there when I want him? He's always unavailable to meet!" Rather than feeling the frustration, Bob piggybacks it onto a thought. The feeling moves from the body to a thought and requires that Bob structure the thought about blaming other people and things. The feeling-thought of frustration is anger.

Frustration lets us know that *we* are out of control, not the situation. When we find ourselves focusing on other people, situations, and experiences, and creating them in our head without actively choosing to, we have piggybacked frustration, which is our indicator to get back into control, by making a different choice. We create thoughts meshed with frustration, and the structure of the thoughts is experienced as thoughts about other people or things. We know that we are creating other people and things when we use words like "he," "she," "they," "you," "them," "those," and so forth. The feeling-thought is anger.

Feeling-Thought: Guilt

In this situation, Jane is a high school senior and is rejected from her first choice in universities. Rather than feeling the sadness and recognizing all her other options, she goes to the past and thinks about all the things she didn't do in high school that could have made a difference in the admissions process to her first-choice university. Here her sadness is piggybacked onto a thought and becomes guilt or regret.

In another example, Linda makes a mistake at work, causing a major project to fall a month behind schedule. Instead of using her sadness to complete the experience and learn from it, she piggybacks the feeling. It is then

40

Emotional Needs →	Natural Feelings →	Feelings = Thoughts
Secure	anxiety	fear
In Control	frustration	anger
Adequate	sadness	guilt

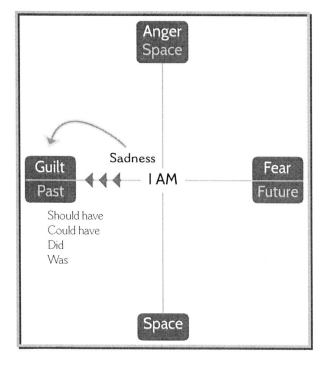

experienced as thoughts with the focus on the past, such as, "I should have asked for help," or "I could have done more research."

This work situation evokes sadness, and Linda piggy-backs it onto a thought. The feeling moves from the body to a thought. The feeling-thought of sadness is guilt or regret.

Sadness lets us know there is no real connection between loss and adequacy. We create thoughts meshed with sadness, and we experience these thoughts in the past. We know we are in the past when we use words like "should have," "could have," "would have," "done," "had," "was," and "did."

These thoughts take us away from the present, where we can use the sadness to complete the experience and keep perspective. The feeling-thought is guilt or regret.

Distortion Is the Foundation

When we leave the Here-Now without conscious choice and go to the future or the past or create other people and experiences, we simultaneously distort ourselves in the negative. The structure of the distortion is that we look at ourselves negatively in an exaggerated way. We lose our capacity to keep a balanced perspective of our strengths and weaknesses.

For example, we may think, "I'm not smart enough," or "I don't have enough education."

We go there directly when we are frustrated with ourselves and turn that frustration into a judgment of ourselves. We go there indirectly when the situation or other people become the basis for the judgment, comparison, or negation.

Natural Feelings

In the Self-Powerment Model, fear, anger, and guilt are not natural, pure feelings. They are distortions of natural feelings that result from the natural feeling being piggybacked onto a thought we create. When feelings and thoughts are meshed together, neither can be used as nature intended. The feelings of anxiety, frustration, and sadness are indicators to let us know that we must do something to reconnect to our balanced state.

Anxiety, frustration, and sadness inherently hold the information that allows us to stay self-powered. When used naturally, thoughts—which by nature limit and define—are also useful and extraordinarily valuable when we can choose when and how to use them. Thinking has tremendous value and can complement the knowledge gained through direct experience. When a feeling becomes a feeling-thought in a nanosecond, however, thinking loses its practical value.

Feelings get piggybacked almost instantaneously. We can use this time-space model to identify which feeling has been piggybacked. We begin by noticing the structure of our thoughts (where we are in time and space). Once we know where we are in time and space, we can shift our attention to the feeling we have piggybacked, experience that feeling, and use it to return to self-powerment.

43

What does it mean to experience a feeling fully? It means to give our full attention to the bodily experience that is occurring at that moment.

When our emotional need for security has been challenged and we find ourselves in the future, we need to shift our focus and be present with the anxiety that is occurring in the body. We feel anxiety in the pit of our stomach.

When we recognize we are focusing on other people, situations, or experiences, we need to shift our attention and be with the feeling of frustration and the resulting physical tension we feel in our body.

When our adequacy need has been challenged and we find ourselves in the past, we need to shift our attention and be with the feeling of sadness that is occurring in the body. We feel sadness in the space in and around our heart.

Any feeling signal that indicates one of our emotional needs is in wobble can take us immediately into our body, where we experience the natural feeling without allowing it to take us out of the Here-Now.

For practical purposes, we have to go to the future to plan, and we have to go back to the past to remember. Sometimes we want to think about other people and things, and sometimes we want to look at our own strengths and weaknesses. When we leave the Here-Now by choice, it serves us. Any other time, it becomes the vehicle for discharging feelings. My experience is that, when asked, most people say that they spend most of their time "flying around out there," not in the Here-Now. It takes an incredible amount of energy to move a feeling onto a thought—energy that could be better used to participate fully in life.

This Is a Model About Choice

If you choose to go to the future to plan, go to the past to remember, or to create other people, situations, or experiences, then that's great. When, however, you find yourself in the future, in the past, creating other people or things, or distorting yourself when you really want to be fully present in the Here-Now, you know you have piggybacked a feeling. Time and space are the pathway to self-powerment. When used as nature intended, they are the roadmaps to the feelings that allow us to stay in the Here-Now, where we find our intuition, wisdom, and creativity. When we are in the Here-Now, we have the choice to take action or not and to make a decision or just wait. Anything we decide is based on true free choice, and the decision is made by drawing on the widest possible multi-sensory database.

Our emotional needs of security, control, and adequacy, and the natural feelings that let us know they are in wobble are inside us, and then life happens. For example, we get a rejection letter, we make a mistake, or we get criticized. These experiences evoke feelings. Once an experience evokes feeling, we need to stay with the feeling in order to stay in the Here-Now. If we observe that it has taken us out of the Here-Now, we can then use it to get back to our balanced state by using time and space and our navigation points.

The situation that evoked the feeling is no longer useful until we can approach it self-powered. We have learned to go in the wrong direction—directing the natural feeling onto a feeling-thought. Now, the situation is overloaded and becomes the stage for the play of our personal drama. The true essence of the experience is lost.

The Lynchmen

We have discussed how piggybacking our feelings takes us out of the Here-Now; however, we have a desire to return there because it is our place of self-powerment. We are kept out of the Here-Now once we leave it by judgments, comparisons, and negations. Negation is used here to indicate that which is not occurring. I call these three terms—judgments, comparisons, and negations—"Lynchmen." The structure of the Lynchmen is to pull our focus to the things being judged, the things being compared, or the things that are not occurring. When we use any of the Lynchmen, we shift our focus away from ourselves in the Here-Now—the only place we can fully participate in life.

Sometimes when people are in my seminar, they compare it to others they have taken, instead of being fully present with the material and experiences presented to them at that moment. In another instance, when I was on a bus tour in beautiful Bali, I sat beside a woman who talked incessantly about her recent trip to England and missed the present experience. In both these instances, these people allowed the Lynchmen to control them.

Essential Principles

In the I Am, we deal with what is; we experience our feelings and use them as nature intended. The natural feelings of anxiety, frustration, and sadness are indicators whose inherent information allows us to act on our environment to stay secure, stay in control, and feel adequate through the process of focus, choice, and clarity. Feeling-thoughts are the structures that keep us away from our place of self-powerment. When we look at them in terms of where they take us in time and space, we can see them clearly and can stop them from occurring.

Three essential principles are illustrated in the Self-Powerment Model:

1. Feelings have a distinct function. Anxiety, frustration, and sadness are internal indicators that our emotional needs are out of balance, and they give us the information about how to act to get back to our balanced state. Other feelings have important functions as well. Like the feelings we discussed, they have not been allowed free and authentic expression in our culture.

Thought is abstraction, which inherently implies
limitation. The whole is too much. There is no
way by which thought can get hold of the whole,
because thought only abstracts; it limits and
defines. And the past from which thought draws
contains only a certain limited amount. The present
is not contained in thought, thus an analysis cannot
cover the moment of analysis.

— David Bohm, *On Dialogue*[4]

Thought takes us out of direct experience. It
takes us to the past or the future, and it shifts focus
to other people, situations, and experiences. It closes
off access to the Here-Now. Thought condenses and
thereby limits experience.

It is in the Here-Now that we are mentally silent.
This silence makes room for awareness to emerge
from our deeper wisdom within.

We have learned to think about almost everything. We think about thoughts, about feelings,
about perceptions, and about behavior. It's remarkable that we spend almost our whole waking life
thinking. We wake up thinking, we take a shower
thinking, we make love thinking, we play golf
thinking, and we work thinking.

There is no doubt that thinking has an important place in our lives; it is immensely valuable

and quite indispensable to a civilized society. But thinking is not life. Life is to be experienced; and when necessary, we can think. We have learned to think all the time and experience occasionally. An example is when a crisis surprises us out of thought. Both Gary Zukav in *The Seat of the Soul*[5] and Eckhart Tolle in *The Power of Now*[6] make this point clearly and powerfully. Often, people need an external crisis to approach the deeper level of reality. This does not have to be the way. We can do this by simply being aware of our option to experience life and awareness.

Beyond thinking is the deeper reality of awareness. We don't avoid our situations by not thinking; we open up to a new and more expansive way of experiencing them.

To approach the deeper reality of life is really nothing more than discovering the value of direct experience and the use of feelings to stay self-powered.

2. Inherent in the experience of feelings is the information we need to stay self-powered. Feelings are felt. They are experienced. "Feelings are our most genuine path to knowledge," says Audre Lorde in *Sister Outsider*.[7] In the Self-Powerment Model, feelings allow us to gain focus, control, and competence.

Feelings allow us to act on our environment, meaning that action is initiated by a feeling.

3. Feelings get piggybacked in a nanosecond. Feeling-thoughts are what we have mistakenly come to know as feelings. When we examine these feeling-thoughts, they are always outside of the I Am. They take us to the future, the past, and other people and things, or they distort us negatively. The key to reconnecting to the original feeling is to find out where we are in time and space by observing the structure of our thought. Where we are in time and space tells us what feeling we have piggybacked. We can then experience the feeling, act on our environment, and stay in the Here-Now. Physicists have used time and space to understand and describe how one object relates to another. In this Self-Powerment Model, time and space are used as references to orient us back to our place of self-powerment. How exciting to use time and space in such a way that ultimately we do not have to use them at all!

It is necessary to identify the structurally learned patterns of our thinking and communication. These patterns hold the information that allows access to direct experience. Where are we in time and space? Are we focusing on others or fragmenting ourselves? Are we judging, comparing, or negating? When we shift our focus to how we structure our thoughts and communication, as opposed to their content, and when we shift from what we are thinking and communicating, a degree of detachment occurs. This detachment allows us to determine whether we have made a choice to pay attention to what we are thinking or talking about or whether we are coming from a structurally learned pattern. *It is by observing our thought structures and what takes us out of the Here-Now that we can then detach from them and choose to return, without thought, to the I Am.* Time and space are our compass points.

Peter Russell in *Waking Up in Time* tells us,

> Our consensus trance is not voluntary; it begins at birth, without our conscious agreement. All authority is surrendered to the parents, family members, and other caretakers, who initially are regarded as omniscient and omnipotent. Induction is not limited to short sessions; it involves years of repeated reinforcement. Clinical therapists would consider it highly unethical to use force, but our cultural hypnotists often do: a slap on the wrist or a severe reprimand for misbehaving. Or perhaps subtler, but equally powerful, emotional pressures: 'I love you only if you think and behave as I tell

you.' Finally, and most significantly, the conditioning is intended to be permanent. It may come from
the very best of intentions, but it is, nevertheless,
meant to have lasting effect on our personalities
and on the way we evaluate the world![8]

Can you imagine our human conditioning being
as thorough as this? The conditioning claims that what
we think is reality. Any evidence to the contrary is dis-
counted, and we continue to maintain our firm convic-
tion that how we think is so.

Thank you to the physicists who brought us awareness of time-space that is not charged with content
like, "She never loved me," "They wouldn't let me in the
school I wanted," and "If I haven't made VP by now, I
never will." Shifting the focus to where thoughts take us
in time and space bypasses all the content and reveals
the feeling that, when we allow ourselves to experience it, brings us back to the Here-Now, our place of
self-powerment. Anyone can do it.

A Tool

The importance of the Journey to Ithaca

We have learned to be so goal-oriented that we actually believe it is acceptable to focus a tremendous amount of our time, energy, and resources to thinking about our goals. In other words, we feel it is worthwhile to spend a great deal of time in the future. We are measured and judged by our achievement of goals. When we finally reach our goals, we know how long the satisfaction lasts. In "Ithaca," the Greek poet C.P. Cavafy[9] challenges us to reconsider this learned focus on goals:

When you start on yore journey to Ithaca
Then pray that the road is long
Full of adventure, full of knowledge
Do not fear the Lestrygonians and the angry
    Cyclops and the angry Poseidon You will never
    meet such as these on your path if your thoughts
    remain lofty
If a fine emotion touches your body and your spirit
You will never meet the Lestrygonians the Cyclops
    and the fierce Poseidon
if you do not carry them within your soul,
if your soul does not raise them up before you.

Then pray that the road is long
That the summer mornings are many
That you will enter parts seen for the first time with
    pleasure,
with such joy!
Stop at Phoenician markets and purchase fine
    merchandise
Mother-of-Pearl and corals, amber and ebony and
    pleasurable
perfumes of all kinds.
Buy as many pleasurable perfumes as you can,
Visit hosts of Egyptian cities
to learn and learn from those who have knowledge.
Always keep Ithaca fixed in your mind
To arrive there is your ultimate goal
But do not hurry the voyage at all
It is better to let it last for long years,
and even to anchor at the isle when you are old rich
    with all that
you have gained on the way not expecting that
    Ithaca will
offer you riches.
Ithaca has given you the beautiful voyage
without her you would have never taken the road
But she has nothing more to give you.
And if you find her poor; Ithaca has not
    defrauded you

With the great wisdom you have gained
With so much experience
You must surely have understood by then what
Ithaca means.

This poem strongly suggests that the only reason to create a goal is to get the wisdom and knowledge gathered along the way to attaining it.

"It is better to let it last for long years, and even to anchor at the isle when you are old rich with all that you have gained on the way not expecting that Ithaca will offer you riches.

Ithaca has given you the beautiful voyage

without her you would have never taken the road."

Since life is always Here-Now, that is where we find the wisdom of life. We can choose to make optimum use of the Here-Now in order to gain the wisdom it holds. The only reason to create a goal is to begin the journey. It is the goal that allows the journey to begin. It is the starting point. The experiences along the way create the path to wisdom.

The traditional way of goal setting is to be at A and to set a goal to get to Z. Then, we do task B and we siphon—that is draw off—a little bit of B to see if we are on target with Z. We do the same thing with C. That is, we siphon off a little of C to see if we are on target with Z. We continue until we reach our goal; and, with a high degree of probability, we will attain something near to it. We evaluate (compare and judge) every experience on whether it is moving us toward goal Z. If the data from the experience do not fit with goal Z, we minimize or discount that data as not valuable. In effect, by doing this, we eliminate the value of all but one or several of the many possibilities.

Note how this applies to the example of a consultant who hired an assistant to help him complete a project. The next week, he met someone eminently more qualified for the project; however, because he had already hired someone, he did not even consider hiring the more qualified person.

In the traditional way of goal setting, we take each experience and evaluate it solely on the basis of whether or not it is going to get us to Z, as defined at point A.

I present this concept visually as follows:

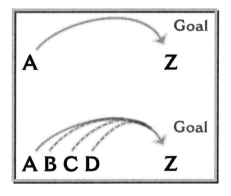

We have learned to believe that if we think of the goal, plan strategies, and create an overall game plan, which we follow precisely, then we will get to Z.

A goal, like any thought or concept, is limiting. I suggest a new way of goal setting. Set goal Z, then fully live A, B, C, and D—which may alter the overall game plan. Fully experience each step along the journey and integrate and utilize what you learned from them. As we begin to actualize the plan, the reality of what we experience along the way can lead to many different outcomes. These unique outcomes from the experiences along the way are our compass pointing to the achievement of the most beneficial goal. We don't change the goal, per se; we just open to greater possibilities to enhance it. When it is wise to change the goal, the knowledge gained from the experiences make that evident.

In this second approach, there is a new value and emphasis placed on creating possibilities from each experience as well as on the achievement of the goal. I represent this visually in the following diagram. There is reward for surprise.

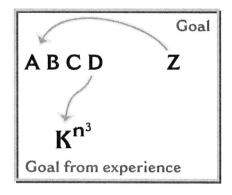

Let's Get Practical

Having a tool is valuable only if we learn how to use it. So, how do we learn to listen differently? How do we learn to listen to the structure of thoughts and communication rather than just to their content?

Did you ever study a foreign language in school? When the teacher began to lecture about pronouns or to teach us about past participles, the pluperfect, and future conditional tenses, that's when I cut class and went across the street for a slice of pizza and an orange soda. If the teacher had explained that tenses orient me in time and pronouns orient me in space and had pointed out the benefits of knowing this, I may have stayed. If I had been told that when I was worrying about my boyfriend's fidelity and was really feeling frustrated at not being able to control that situation, I would have learned something valuable. When we listen for tenses and pronouns, we begin to hear where we are in time and space.

We can use our orientation in time and space to identify what feeling we have piggybacked and can use that information to reconnect to the feeling, experience that feeling, and use it to get back to the Here-Now.

By referring to the Self-Powerment Model above, you can see that once you have identified where you are in time and space, there are two arrows that point down.

Emotional Needs	Natural Feelings	Feelings – Thoughts	Sample – Situations
Secure	anxiety	fear	rejections
In Control	frustration	anger	mistakes
Adequate	sadness	guilt	criticisms

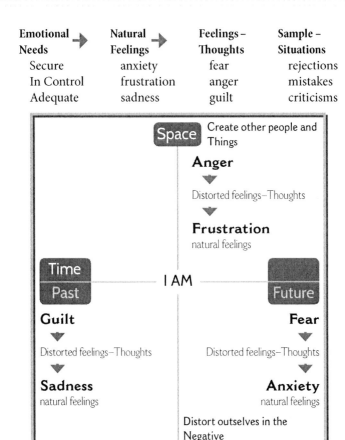

The top arrow indicates what the feeling-thought is. The bottom arrow indicates what the natural feeling is. To deepen our understanding of how the Model works, let's practice with some sentence structures.

Here is a sentence that we hear often at work: "You should have gotten it to me last week."

Here is a sentence that we hear often in relationships: "You should have asked for my opinion before you made that decision."

Refer to the Model. Where is "you"? It is on the space line axis of creating other people and things. Now, what is the feeling-thought? It is anger. And what is the feeling? Frustration!

Now, where is "should have" on the model? It is on the time line axis in the past. The feeling-thought is guilt, and the feeling is sadness.

Thus, the way to experience thoughts of "You should have gotten it to me last week" or "You should have called last night" in the Here-Now is to feel your frustration and sadness, respectively.

Here are two more examples: "I am not going to be able to lose that weight—never!" And "I can't get this done by Thursday." "By Thursday" and "never" take us on the time axis to the future. The feeling-thought is fear. The feeling is anxiety. The way to experience thoughts of "I can't get it done by Thursday" or "I am not going to lose weight—never" in the Here-Now is to feel your anxiety and focus your attention in the Here-Now.

When we piggyback a feeling onto a thought, the content of the communication becomes the focus, taking us away from the feeling evoked in the Here-Now.

Let's try two more examples: "I would have received the raise if I had worked harder," and "My girlfriend wouldn't have broken up with me if I had tried harder to be a good boyfriend." As a word used in both examples, where is "would have" on the Model? It is on the time axis in the past. The feeling-thought is guilt, and the feeling sadness. The Lynchmen comparison is seen in "worked harder" and "tried harder." So the grounded and centered way to experience this sentence is simply to feel your sadness.

Let's now elaborate on the situation in which Rachel invites her boyfriend over for the evening, which was mentioned previously. He's late and then very late. We've all been in this type of situation, just change the names and address. Rachel's boyfriend is Tom; and because Rachel is not accustomed yet to observing her thoughts, we will add her good friend Connie, who will do this for her.

RACHEL: It's already eight-fifteen. Tom was supposed to be here at eight o'clock. He's always late. Why can't he be on time for once?

CONNIE: Come on, Rachel, you really can't say "always." I know you are anxious about whether he is coming or not.

RACHEL: Okay then, sometimes. If he's not here soon, the steak will get dry, and the vegetables will be overcooked.

CONNIE: You're focused on the dinner. I know you are frustrated that he's not here already. Let's call him at home to at least see if he's left. If he's not there, we can try his cell.

[Rachel makes the two telephone calls, but there is no answer.]

RACHEL: Connie, it's eight-thirty. Now, I'm really getting upset. The dinner is ruined for sure.

CONNIE: I know you're disappointed that he's not here by now. You're really a great cook. It's sad to have worked so hard to prepare him a nice meal and not have him here to enjoy it. Hey, this is a good time to look at that batch of pictures of the two of you that you just picked up.

RACHEL: I hate him. I need to find another boyfriend. He's so insensitive to who I am and what I need.

CONNIE: Look, Rachel, I know you are really frustrated and probably feeling out of control now. Remember our lunch last week when you were telling me about all the wonderful things he has done for you lately? Let's keep this in perspective.

RACHEL: If I marry him, what if he's late all the time? That will drive me crazy, Connie.

CONNIE: Hey, you're way into the future now, talking of some possibility.

RACHEL: Connie, now it's nine. What if something happened to him? What if he got into a car accident? He could be hurt somewhere.

CONNIE: I know you're feeling anxious, Rachel. Try his cell one more time, and then try calling his sister. She may have an explanation.

RACHEL: No, I'm tired of playing detective here. I hate him. I don't care if he's dead.

CONNIE: Slow down, Rachel. That's serious judgment. Let's wait and see what the reason is for his being late.

[Rachel is adamant.]

RACHEL: I just know that he's met another woman. She's probably younger and more beautiful than I am. I bet he's with her right now.

CONNIE: Now, you're back to being anxious and frustrated again. Chances are there's a perfectly reasonable explanation.

[It's nine-fifteen. Rachel's fears have completely taken over at this stage.]

RACHEL: Oh, my God. I'll never get married and have children. How will I be able to deal with the loneliness?

CONNIE: I know you must be feeling insecure now. Please try not to take it personally. All we know is that Tom is late.

[At ten, the doorbell rings. Rachel runs to the door and flings it open. There is Tom, breathless and covered with mud.]

TOM: You'll never believe what happened. As I was coming into the city, I took what I thought would be a shortcut because I didn't want to be late. Well, I got a flat tire on a country road. I forgot to recharge the battery on my cell this morning and had to wait an hour before somebody came along to give me a ride. He was a great guy. He was even nice enough to drive me right here. With all that rain and mud, I must look a mess. I'm so sorry, honey.

Now, let's move from the home to the workplace so we can see how flexible this Model is in application. Here is a challenging conversation between a manager and her employee. This conversation is written verbatim. As you read, try to identify where the manager and employee are in time and space and determine what the feeling-thoughts are as well as the corresponding feeling for each.

Employee/Manager Interaction

EMPLOYEE: I'm very frustrated that not everyone is taking this project seriously. It's an insult to management that when we ask for something to be done, it doesn't get done. I admit some people are doing more than their share of the work, but

these few can't pull most of the load. I'm afraid
I'll never be able to get anything done if you don't
make these people listen to me and make them
do the work. I don't know if they're lazy or just
can't organize their time or if they're not team
players, but it's the same people all the time.
[Here's a well-meaning, sound, and typical
human resource response from the manager.]

MANAGER: Let's look at this project that you're
trying to get done in the total context of what
they're doing. I know that some people have
different work pressures than others. People
have different field sizes; we have given them
different assignments. What I'm hearing from
the team leaders is that there's nobody out there
sitting on their hands waiting for their next
assignment. They're all pressured with multiple
priorities, and what I suggest is that you ask
some of the people who have not been able to
get this project done what their plan is. Have
the team leaders call them in and say, "You seem
to be struggling with getting this project done,
and we wanted to have it done by the end of the
year; it doesn't look like that's going to happen
for you. What's your plan? When do you think
you might be able to get it done? And how can I
support you in that?"

Now, let's look at what this dialogue sounds like when the manager is a practitioner of the Self-Powerment Model and focuses on staying in the present moment and grounding and centering her employee. It represents a whole new way of communicating.

EMPLOYEE: I'm very frustrated that not everyone is taking this project seriously. It's an insult to management that when we ask for something to be done, it doesn't get done. Some people do more than their share of the work. I'm afraid I'll never be able to get anything done if you don't make these people listen to me and make them do the work. I don't know if they're lazy or just can't organize their time or they're not team players, but it's the same people all the time.

MANAGER: Chris, you say you're feeling frustrated. Talk to me about that.

[Note how the manager focuses Chris on her feeling of frustration, centering her back on herself.]

EMPLOYEE: Totally. I feel overwhelmed with frustration. It's just—I can't get anything done. No one helps me; people are not doing their job. I give them directives, Betsy, but they don't follow up.

MANAGER: So, sounds like you're out of control.

[The manager labels them emotional; I need for Chris to check herself.]

EMPLOYEE: Totally.

MANAGER: What can I do to help you with this?

EMPLOYEE: You have to talk to them, make them listen to me.

MANAGER: Rather than talk to them, how can I help you?

[Once again, the manager takes Chris back to the Here-Now with the focus being on Chris.]

EMPLOYEE: I have no idea. I don't know.

MANAGER: Yes, you do. Focus on you—not on them. You're very capable, Chris. You can do this.

[The manager gives Chris the acknowledgment that she is in control and capable of identifying solutions.]

EMPLOYEE: Well, they could've held a meeting last Monday to discuss the project, but they just didn't do it. They could've gotten together for a coffee break in the afternoon and discussed it after I had a meeting with a few of them.

MANAGER: Look, those possibilities don't exist any-more—they're in the past. It's sad and frustrat-ing when projects don't go well. Let's look at what's happening now—and what we can do now—to get these people going.

[The manager listens to the structure of communication and identifies that Chris is in the past ("could have") and is focused on other people. She also identifies Chris's feelings of sadness and frustration.]

EMPLOYEE: But, Betsy, you don't understand. We'll never meet the deadline. They're never going to get it done. Every time we discuss what has to be done, they don't listen. They don't follow up, especially John; he's just totally ridiculous.

MANAGER: Listen, you're way out there—way into the future. What's going on now? It sounds like you're frustrated and anxious about doing a good job. [The manager, still observing the structure of Chris's communication, identifies that she is in the future ("never") and is still focused on other people and things ("John" and "they"). She acknowledges Chris's feelings of frustration and anxiety.]

EMPLOYEE: You know, you're right. I really am feeling anxious about how you're going to view me, my job, and everyone else, as a matter of fact. I just—I don't want anyone to think I'm not capable.

MANAGER: Hey! It's really okay. Let's work together to look at what you can do with your resources right now. Once you've identified this, let me know if I can help you somehow.

This dialogue illustrates how we can use personal choice to help ground and center individuals in the Here-Now. We can help them see that they can choose where they are in time and space and the benefits of choosing to be in the Here-Now.

When they are in the future, they have piggybacked anxiety and can chose to use that anxiety to focus on getting the task done. When they are creating other people and things, they have piggybacked frustration and can use the frustration to get back in control so that energy is available to them to deal with the current reality. When they are in the past, they have piggybacked sadness and can use the sadness to experience closure and come back to the present, feeling adequate to get the task done.

In his book *The Dancing Wu Li Masters*,[10] Gary Zukav quotes David Finkelstein, a professor of physics, who writes, "Symbols (language) do not follow the same rules as experience. In short the problem is not in the language, the problem is the language."

The problem is, indeed, language when we lack awareness of how we structure its content. When language is used as a tool to move us to the Here-Now, it becomes the vehicle to connect us to feelings, which are the pathway to self-powerment.

How we structure what we say, not what we say, becomes the crucial element in communication. Does our communication keep us focused in the Here-Now—in the I Am? Does it contain dialogue in which what you say is the stimulus for my response, and my response is the stimulus for what you say instead of what I say being created by what I think?

When we begin to hear the feelings embedded in the content and can discern them, we can use these feelings as nature intended—to keep us in the present.

Any Questions?

Many people who have taken my seminar, and others who have just heard about it, have questions they want answered. Here are some of the most frequently asked questions and my answers. The questions are written verbatim.

Q: When you are in the I Am, aren't you self-centered, impulsive, and caring only about yourself?

A: No. When you live in the I Am, you know intuitively that you are connected to everyone. Actually, your entire experience of self changes dramatically. It is here that you can detach from the personal image of yourself and experience the universal energy, which integrates all of us. In the Here-Now, impulsiveness does not exist because the experience of the centered present is all that there is. The connectedness of experience is found in the I Am. To care only about yourself involves separation from others.

Q: How can you be in the I Am in the workplace, which is so goal-oriented?

A: In the I Am, you understand that the only reason to create a goal is to get the wisdoms and learning from the experience. Once an organization realizes that supporting the people who work there to come into the Here-Now allows them to utilize productively the learning from their hands-on experience, the organization will refocus on creating possibilities as a critical step to increasing profitability. Create possibilities, and profitability follows.

Q: How can I remember to stay in the I Am?

A: In the Self-Powerment Model, remembering means unlearning the patterns that keep you out of the I Am. Since there are countless content patterns, it makes much more sense to reposition yourself using time and space. Vigilant attention to where you are in time and space allows you to refocus your energy onto your feelings and use them to stay in the present. Checking in with yourself frequently every day, asking the question, "Where am I?" is a great way to start.

Q: I don't believe it works.

A: Don't believe me? Try it for yourself! Let your experience provide your own evidence. Try it for a few weeks and notice if there is any change in your experience of yourself, your relationships, and your environment. As with any new tool, you have

74

to practice and get the experience while practicing to really see how it works. What better tool to develop an expertise with than a tool that allows you to stay self- powered?

Q: If I am in the I Am, I'll probably just want to have fun and live for today.

A: When you live in the I Am, you know that each day is a precious gift to experience and from which to learn. When you are in the I Am, you're connected to the eternal present and the vastness of your internal universe. Life becomes something for which you are deeply grateful.

Q: How can I stay in the I Am when life dictates that I must think ahead to be prepared for the unexpected?

A: When you live in the I Am, full participation in your experience allows you most of the information needed to deal with the unexpected. Full partici- pation in the moment prepares you for the unex- pected. For example, a woman I know needed to sell her house but had nowhere to go to live. Once she put up the "for sale" sign and started to manifest the experience of selling her house by talking about it with others, a wonderful, surprising opportunity opened up that was helpful not only to her but also to a friend and the children of both families.

Q: If I'm in the I Am in a relationship or work environment and a partner or a coworker who has
taken your seminar on living in the Here-Now
isn't, what can I say to get them back?

A: The key question for helping someone to become
aware of where they are in time and space is,
"Where are you—now?" It is essential to shift
from a focus on the content of the communication
to where that content is taking you in time and
space. Re-referencing yourself or others allows an
altered perspective, which then helps the individual to get back to the present moment where
energy is focused.

Q: When do you see yourself beyond the I Am?

A: When you're in the I Am, there is no beyond.
There is an entirely unique relationship to the
present because you know that is all there is. You
respect and honor your day because that day is the
gift of living.

Q: When using the I Am process in coaching and
development, how can we clearly set expectations?

A: The key expectation is that people participate
fully in their experience. This framework allows
all individuals to experience self-powerment,
which includes accountability, responsibility, and
integrity as intrinsic elements of how they relate

in their lives. Expectations that are set for the future, without choice, take our energy from the present. Choosing both to create an expectation and to participate fully in every experience allows a whole new approach for utilizing expectations as the means of ongoing learning.

Q: Do you need a certain requirement to teach this to others?

A: The only requirement to teach being in the Here-Now is being aware with vigilant attention to where you are in time and space. Be a role model for living in the present with your energy focused inside yourself. Using feelings as nature intended—as the pathway to self-powerment—is the most effective tool available to you. When you are in the Here-Now, you automatically invite others to join you there. When you are in the Here-Now, you can't help but be a teacher of present-moment living.

Q: How can I manage work and family and have time for me?

A: When you are in the I Am, you have more than enough time and energy to address what life presents to you. You aren't dissipating your energy by worrying about the future or regretting and reworking something in the past. You aren't giving your power away to other people and events. You are focusing on the priorities that enable you to feel secure, in control, and adequate. When you use your energy to accomplish the task at hand, predictably you accomplish it with efficiency and creativity. Remember, you must take care of yourself first. This isn't selfishness but healthy self-care. Then, you still have more than enough time and energy to give to others—and you will give it cleanly and without the negative charge of resentment.

Q: So often people come to me, looking for answers; and since there are infinite possibilities, how can I help them to see they already have the solution and that my feedback is just one possibility?

A: By not giving an answer, you insist that people look within themselves for the answer. When you give an answer, it is your definition of reality that they are buying. Let people discover the answer themselves by helping them to re-reference themselves to the place where they will know the answer through their own resources.

Q: What will happen when we are all capable of remaining in the I Am?

A: When we move to the next level of consciousness, where people's primary motivation is to be of service and where people feel self-powered to behave in ways that are inspired by their intuition as well as by reason, we can focus on addressing problems as paradoxes and moving toward the right relationship with what is. How that manifests is totally unknown and is a wonderful muse as we create possibilities.

Q: What about the search for new beginnings?

A: Always keep Ithaca fixed in your mind ... "To arrive there is your ultimate goal; But do not hurry the voyage at all." New beginnings become the nature of what is so. Creating new possibilities becomes the focus when you are present. New beginnings are new possibilities coming into being. They are one and the same.

Q: How do you deal with someone who is consistently negative when you're trying to be in the I Am?

A: When people are being negative, they are saying what isn't—not what is. You can help them by encouraging them to refocus on what is so. Help them deal with that rather than create the negative. It is highly probable that they have piggybacked a feeling and have discharged all their energy, so your gift is to refocus them onto the place where they can acknowledge and use their feelings to get back to being self-powered. Just keep asking, "What is so?" When you have compassion, you respond with concern and caring rather than reacting and becoming defensive.

Q: How do I apply the principle to an individual who is passive-aggressive and does not acknowledge any feelings or actions?

A: Clearly that person is feeling frustrated and out of control. They are also feeling a tremendous amount of anxiety that they have piggybacked onto behavior. Labeling their feelings is a good way to begin. Remember, when people are self-powered, they relate to others with respect. When emotional needs are in wobble, those needs must be addressed, and that person is only trying, albeit unsuccessfully, to experience security and control in his or her life. Speak to those emotional concerns.

Q: How can you take principles of I Am to upwardly change the organization from a top-down to a bottom-up one?

A: When you are in the I Am, you have more than enough time and energy. You are connected to the place of accountability, responsibility, and integrity. As you live in the present, your relationship to your job, your performance, and your team changes dramatically. You role-model the new behaviors, and, by doing this, you influence your coworkers and leaders. There is an increase in passion and productivity, which is clearly demonstrable in the bottom line. Everyone becomes accountable for creating profitability, but not necessarily by rigidly adhering to the procedures and methods created in the old paradigm. When you are in the I Am, you know that the obstacles to peak performance are not other people. It is the structures that they are forced to work in that inhibits their ability to be productive, creative, innovative, and, above all, in service to the other employees within the company.

Q: Is the I Am the only solution to all our daily problems?

A: There are many ways to deal with daily problems. Being in the Here-Now is one of the most practical since it doesn't cost any money or take extra time. All it requires is that we open our awareness to where we are in time and space so we can access and use feelings as nature intended. Being present allows us to connect to the gateway through which creative solutions become possible. In the I Am, we can see that perhaps we're asking the wrong questions, that something what we thought was a problem really wasn't, or that a problem itself can be restructured to be seen as an opportunity.

Q: As society moves at an ever-increasing pace, will it be possible to live in the I Am all the time?

A: Actually, it is essential to be in the Here-Now as the pace of society increases. In the Here-Now, there are infinite possibilities at any given moment, which allow for change to be experienced as natural. The I Am is the state where change exists and occurs most naturally.

Q: How can I use the I Am tool at home when I have a wife or husband who always reminds me of the future?

A: People who live in the future are people who have learned to piggyback their feeling of anxiety. By using anxiety naturally to focus and participate fully in life, a person continually creates the experiences necessary to take care of the future. For example, you can help your wife by assisting her to refocus on the Here-Now. Ask her, "What is happening—now?" Help her to connect with her present-moment feeling and support her in taking the time now to act to feel secure. The same holds true for the husband.

Q: If everything is relative, how do you know what is the real truth?

A: The real truth exists in this moment. It is the eternal present that provides us with the information that we need to know to understand what is so.

Q: How can you just disregard the past if all that you know is learned through experience?

A: When you fully participate in an experience, you take the wisdom and lessons learned from that experience and incorporate them into your knowing of what is so. It is the integration of the knowing, rather than the content, that provides the wisdom from experience. The learning takes place through the experience, not because of it.

Q: How do you respond to a child's anxiety, such as is expressed in, "I'm really nervous about the test tomorrow"?

A: Allow the child to experience the anxiety. Talk about it, draw it, dance it, and paint it. Anxiety is the feeling that allows the child to focus and be fully in the experience. Of course, knowing the test material is essential. The ability to be clear and focused allows that knowledge to be turned into a successful outcome.

Q: How can I bring my thoughts back to the Here-Now when I'm already deep in fear?

A: One way is ask someone for help. Other people are a key resource when you are not present. Let them listen, and allow them to identify where you are and label your feeling. You can then shift your attention onto the feeling and use it to get back to your natural emotional state of security. Another way is to begin a journal. Just put your pencil on the paper and write. What your internal universe says is a key to getting back to feeling emotionally secure.

Q: Why don't you talk to our manager to give us some time each day to practice being present?

A: When you have practiced and experience how much more efficient, productive, and creative you are, you know that it is something you must do, just like eating or drinking. It is not up to the manager to give you the time in which to do it. It is your life and your choice to live self-powered.

Q: How can you remain in the I Am in traffic?

A: When you're in traffic, you're in traffic, and that is *what is so*. Most people want to be somewhere else: in the future and out of the traffic. They dissipate their energy by leaving the present; but you can choose to take this time, this present moment, to listen to music, muse on possibilities, admire nature, or enjoy being with yourself. It is a time the universe has given you to participate in your life in a way that keeps you self-powered.

Q: How long does it usually take to realize that you're not in the Here-Now?

A: Awareness is required, and practice is the key that opens the gateway to self-powerment. The more you practice, the more the awareness of where you are in time and space becomes integrated with how you live your life. Once you are in the I Am, feelings can again be natural indicators to stay grounded and centered.

Q: How can the person in the I Am help his or her partner stay out of the past?

A: When a person is in the past without choosing to be, it is because they have piggybacked the feeling of sadness onto a thought. Identify where the person is in time and what feeling has been piggybacked. Create opportunities for that person to experience their adequacy in the present.

Q: How do you get into the I Am when a past experience you thought you put closure to shows up again and again?

A: In his book *The Seat of the Soul*, Gary Zukav[11] says that we are in the earth's school, and that the universe is quite compassionate, giving us repeated experiences until the lesson has been learned. The notion is that maybe there are still many leanings that will help you obtain the wisdom you need. Be grateful for the opportunity to learn and grow. We need to participate fully in our experiences, not judge whether they are the "right" ones for us to have. Actually, we can say that we repeat the automatic connection of the feeling to the thought. We are not aware of this connection. When we truly become clear about how we feel and can consciously connect the feeling to the repetitious thought, the non-reality of the thought content becomes apparent.

Q: I thought that we were supposed to share our feelings.

A: Feelings are natural indicators to let us know if our emotional needs are in wobble and if we must act on our environment to stay present. Feelings are yours to use to stay self-powered. They are internal and individual, and it is a matter of choice whether you share them or not. They are the pathway to self-powerment, the pathway to connect to the soul.

There are many more questions, and I can guarantee that answers evolve at the same rate as our consciousness evolves to receive them.

Here-Now and The Bottom Line

A Look at the Self-Powerment Model in the Workplace

The Self-Powerment Model is applicable to so very many areas: conflict resolution, effective communication skills, stress management, parenting skills, creative problem-solving, personal coaching, and many more. In this chapter, the business arena is discussed as one example of its many applications.

These times of growing uncertainty and escalated change bring both higher risk and demand for peak performance. To survive and adapt in the business arena, we need to do something different. Einstein told us that we couldn't solve problems at the same level on which they were created.[12]

Now is the time to move to the next generation of business effectiveness. This involves seeing our world and ourselves differently. There is clear evidence from the hard sciences of physics, biology, and neurology, as well as evidence from the fields of psychology, linguistics, and organizational development, that confirms that we utilize only a small portion of our innate intelligence and creativity.

> The intellectual assets of most companies are probably worth at least three or four times the company's tangible book value, yet no CEO I know could honestly claim to be actually utilizing more than 20 percent of his or her firm's intellectual capital base. Can you imagine the fate of any CEO who could only manage 20 percent utilization rate in his or her production capacity, inventory, efficiency, or any other traditional index of performance? I can't even bear thinking about that. Yet in this, the most important wealth creating area of all, a 20 percent efficiency rate is considered normal, inevitable, and acceptable. Well, it isn't.
> —Matthew J. Kiernan, *The Eleven Commandments of 21st Century Management*[13]

Why do we use only a fraction of our intellectual capital? Because we think we already know most of what there is to know. We are like the proverbial blind man touching the leg of an elephant and believing it to be a tree trunk.

Until now, innate intelligence and creativity have been grossly underutilized, mainly because of the insistence on quantitative measurement and rewards based solely on direct financial results. To access this innate intelligence and creativity, which enhance the bottom line, we must expand our vision to see beyond the limitation of what can be measured quantitatively. We must open ourselves more fully to information that is qualitatively valuable. When we do not limit ourselves to thought, we become receptive to the multidimensional sensory experience in which intelligence and creativity reside. This information is in the Here-Now and is open to all employees.

To reiterate, there are two quite distinct databases— one from thought and one from direct experience. We have come to believe that thinking is the most powerful source of information for strategic planning, marketing, sales, and other business activities. Indeed, we have been taught to think about everything. In this information age, we believe quantity and organization of information compiled through discussion and strategic planning to be the highest form of possibility for innovation and successful outcomes. The data that is experienced from thought, however, only continues to add more quantity to existing structures.

We need to include information from the Here-Now. In the Here-Now, time can expand, collapse, and curve. Space is full or empty, can leap across continents, or contain a universe in a grain of sand. Knowing this, consider the possibilities of what can be done when we break free from the absolute definition of time and space.

When we let time and space blend into a unified time-space, we discover the boundless creative possibilities of multidimensional experience within each employee.

How does this link with the Self-Powerment Model? Strict focus on the goal and the gathering of only quantitative evidence to verify achievement minimize the value and learning found within each experience. To miss the importance of learning from each experience and the opportunities to do so is to significantly reduce the creation of possibilities for enhanced goal achievement. The next step is evident.

Drop rigid adherence to the goal, and the creation of possibilities becomes the natural experience. Each experience along the way opens to new possibilities that are cumulative and exponential and, when acted upon, improve results. Living in the Here-Now is the mechanism to achieve this vital expansion.

Consider the following benefits of practicing this new way of being in the workplace:

1. Employees have more energy. When employees are in the Here-Now, not regretting things that are in the past, worrying about the future, or shifting their focus outside themselves to others and things, their energy is focused in the present. Since they are no longer using their energy to put feelings onto thoughts—and this happens in many instances all

day long—this energy is now available directly to the task at hand.

2. Employees are clear and focused on their work in the now. When employees feel secure, in control, and adequate, they naturally use feelings to maintain clarity and focus since feelings are the tools that nature gives us so that we can maintain balance, clarity, and focus. Feelings contain tremendous information and energy, both of which can be accessed for productive and healthy purposes.

3. Employees are resilient to change. On the whole, organizations have done remarkably well in adapting to technological changes. What is required now is for employees to experience this same adaptability in their lives. When we are in the Here-Now, we experience infinite possibilities, which give us greater resources to be resilient to change. We are not trying to hold on to the past and cling to former ways and traditions, nor are we spending energy projecting or worrying about the future. Instead, we are comfortable with what is happening in the moment.

4. Employees have more productive relationships. When employees no longer create judgments, comparisons, and negations, and live in the Here-Now, they are able to interact in a way that allows a

new level of combined intelligence. This has never occurred before on a large scale.

The person who figures out how to harness the collective genius of the people in his or her organization is going to blow the competition away.
—Walter Wriston, CEO, former President, Citicorp/Citibank[14]

When employees are present with each other in the Here-Now, they experience a qualitative difference in their relationships. We already know that when individuals combine in common purpose to achieve a goal and work as a synergistic team, the sum of their energy is more than the sum of the individual energies involved. We have already accepted that in this situation that two plus three equals more than 5. If these same individuals combine in common purpose to achieve a goal while in the Here-Now, they form a new level of intelligence, which is called **conjoined intelligence**. Conjoined intelligence takes place when the joining of the intelligence of a group of individuals creates a new form of intelligence.

5. Employees are innovative, and creative solutions are found as needed. Any profound act of creation

comes out of the state of being in the Here-Now. All of us can choose to be in the I Am. When employees are able to use time and space to access this place, they tap into their creative potential. We know that we are holding the creative tension between goal achievement and possibilities when we have the qualitative evidence that employees are more energetic, clear, focused, and resilient to change; have more productive work relationships; and are able to solve problems creatively. The quantitative evidence of the successful application of the Self-Powerment Model is found in a healthier bottom line.

Musings: Going Deeper

If you have read this far to get the information necessary to integrate the principles of the Self-Powerment Model into your everyday life, you have certainly met the expectation of this author. However, if like me, you have become deeply intrigued with the possibilities of this shift to the Here-Now, I share some personal musings for your reflection. I welcome you to use them as starting points for your own musing. My suggestion is that you read only one muse at a time, reflect on it, and use the pages provided at the end of this chapter to record your own impressions.

To muse is to speculate voluntarily. When we muse, we take something that speaks to us, and we willingly let go of the boundaries of the limited thinking mind as we give ourselves over to the process of letting our inner compass guide us along. To muse is to speculate about possibilities. As such, it has the potential to expand our awareness of reality—of what is so. The question "What if this is so?" triggers many possible implications. To muse is to have no attachment to outcome, nor is outcome an intrinsic part of musing.

It is of great importance that the general public be
given an opportunity to experience—consciously
and intelligently—the efforts and results of scientific research. It is not sufficient that each result be
taken up, elaborated and applied by a few specialists
in the field: Restricting the body of knowledge to
a small group deadens the philosophical spirit of a
people and leads to spiritual poverty.

—Albert Einstein[15]

When I am in the I Am, I'm open to that place where
time and space are relative and where the information
now known in quantum physics can be experienced in
everyday life. Concepts like complementarity, non-local
influence, and wave-particle duality have all emerged
as helpful tools for lay folk to live with awareness. The
intuitive nature of quantum physics can be achieved
through the doorway of the I Am—where they are no
longer concepts, but experiences.

Einstein did not set out to prove anything about the
nature of our minds. His interest was in physics.
The fact that he did illustrate something of importance about the way that we structure our perceptions is indicative of an inevitable trend toward the
merger of physics and psychology.

—Gary Zukav, The Dancing Wu Li Masters[16]

One of the most exciting parts of the Self-Powerment Model is the intrinsic connection between psychology and physics. In order for me to appreciate this connection, I had to change the domain in which I saw physics. Instead of complex mathematical formulas presented in unfathomable symbols and equations, physics now expanded to the study of relationships, relativity of concepts, and possibilities. For example, the uncertainty principle states that we cannot observe something without changing it. There is no such thing as the independent observer who can stand on the sideline and watch nature run its course without influencing it. This reality has a great impact on our reliance on measurement as the most powerful tool for assessing real change.

Ken Wilber in *The Spectrum of Consciousness* states that "the point then, is not to confuse the world as it is with the world as it is measured into space, time, objects, classes, delineations, boundaries, limits, particulars, universals, individuals, generals, or categories of any type or kind—for the simple reason that all measurement is a product of thought not reality; just as for example, wood is not actually composed of inches but is only conventionally and mentally measured or divided into very arbitrary slots called 'inches.'"[17]

What this means is that much of the quantitative data generated by the business world is really a product of what individual people choose to see and therefore choose to measure and therefore choose to act upon—as if it were so.

Does this mean that quantitative measurement draws arbitrary conclusions because it depends totally upon the context created by the measurer?

In the current business context of Enron, World-Com, and Arthur Andersen, to name but a few companies, drawing any conclusion based upon the quantitative financial picture painted of the Enrons and WorldComs is impossible or at best highly dangerous. It is not only a matter of what the individuals painting the picture choose to see but also what they wish the viewer to see, regardless of the truth of the ultimate picture.

When we think about something, we move in linear time; therefore, we cannot experience the present.

> The present is not contained in thought. Thus, an analysis cannot actually cover the moment of analysis.
> —David Bohm, *On Dialogue*[18]

If we are paying attention to our thinking, we are not experiencing, and we can only experience in the I Am.

> Surely, to be creative means to be in the state in which truth can come into being. And truth can come into being only when there is a complete cessation of the thought process.
> —J. Krishnamurti[19]

We have learned to think about everything. Common wisdom cautions us to think before we speak, to think before we act. But as long as we're thinking, we're not experiencing. Take a small boy playing on the kitchen floor with a pot and a spoon. He loves playing with the pot and spoon and isn't thinking, "Last week, I wasn't as good a banger," or "Next week, if I practice, I will be a better banger," or "Sarah is a better banger than I," or "I'll never be a good banger." He is just banging, loving it, and learning about life. He's learning about how other people respond to his banging. He may discover, "Oops, if I bang too hard, I make a dent in the pot." Through that experience he learns about pressure and force. He's learning a lot about reality without thinking about it.

Thinking has created the belief system that truth can be observed and measured—that it is somehow independent of the person observing the "truth." Quantum physics has now called that reality into question. Thinking is very useful for practical purposes. It also allows abstraction, which is necessary to create much of the technology we use every day. Abstraction, a subset of reality, is both useful and necessary, but not sufficient for allowing access to direct experience.

When we are in the Here-Now, we know the true meaning of nonattachment.

In this state of consciousness, the true meaning of non-attachment is apparent … It is simply that I am no longer attached to the need for things or events to be a certain way. I have let go of the belief that what goes on around me determines whether or not I am content.

—Peter Russell, *Waking Up in Time*[20]

We learn to experience life by creating an expectation of how we want things to be and then comparing the reality of what is to that expectation. Rarely do we just participate in reality as it is.

When we are attached to something—someone or an outcome—we cannot fully enter into an experience. When we buy our new dream car, we get attached to it. When we teach, we get attached to our students. When we apply for a job, we are attached to getting it. When we fall in love, we get attached to our lover. Attachments come in the form of thought processes whose content sustain the need for the attachment. So in truth, we are not allowing ourselves to participate fully in the experience and address whatever the experience brings. We take energy from the experience to create the attachment. We pay a high price for attachments: we drain ourselves of energy. Since we create the attachment in the first place, we think we can control all the variables associated with it. When we begin to live the experience, we control only ourselves; therefore, the experience must be different.

> In the Here-Now there is an intuitive understanding
> of the nature of paradox. However; as long as para-
> dox is treated as a problem, it can never be resolved.
> —David Bohm, *On Dialogue*[21]

When we experience life as a paradox, a whole new relationship to value emerges. So instead of looking at laziness as something to eliminate, we can see intrinsic value in it as a balance to the work ethic. If we responded to that ethic all the time, we would experience stress and eventual burnout. Paradox, then, allows for each part of life to be of service to the overall whole.

In her book, *The Quantum Self,* Dana Zohar[22] postulates that the origin of consciousness has a physical basis. She speaks about a state in which all the neurons vibrate in unison when at a certain frequency and calls this the blackboard of consciousness. Vibration is very difficult to notice when we are busy thinking. It has such a physical basis that a person must be "in tune" with the vibration to experience it. When we think without choice, we create static interference, which totally cuts off our ability to experience the rhythm of the universe both internally and externally.

When in the I Am, we experience our resonance with the environment, with other humans, and with ourselves. Can rhythm and vibrations possibly be the origin of both spirit and matter?

In *The Spell of the Sensuous* David Abram states, "It is not writing per se, but phonetic writing and the Greek alphabet in particular, that enables the abstraction of previously ephemeral qualities like "goodness" and "justice" from their inherence in situations promoting them to a new realm independent of the flux of ordinary experience."[23]

How can inherent qualities like goodness and justice be abstracted out of an experience? Before there was language, if I wanted to describe or relate to you my experience of my cat, the actual cat had to be present. Once we create the word cat, which stands for the actual cat, then my actual cat no longer needs to be part of present experience for me to talk about it.

Before there was language, if a man took a piece of bread because his children were starving before his eyes, this situation had a very different meaning than the word "stealing" has in modern-day law.

Language allows concepts like goodness and justice to be independent of what is happening Here-Now. Consequently, language cannot communicate the reality of what is so, only the abstraction of that reality.

Conclusion

Exploration of awareness, how to access direct experience in the Here-Now, has been studied since ancient times, particularly through the writing and meditation practices of spiritual mystics and Eastern religions. Humans have long been in search of that state in which we can be truly and fully ourselves—in all our glory and potentiality.

Today, as never before, an increasingly large number of individuals all over the world are searching for ways to experience living in the Here-Now. We know that the wisdom gained from accessing and utilizing direct experience is no longer a luxury; in fact, it is requisite for our survival as a human species. How fitting that the modern science of quantum physics wed with modern psychology has pointed us to another gateway into the Here-Now at this pivotal time in human evolution. This gateway is universally available to us all—right here, right now.

Once we witness how we almost always use time and space to structure our thoughts and language in ways that keep us out of the Here-Now, we can then consciously choose to reverse this process. By changing the structure of our language to the I Am, we change and expand our experience of reality. If we pay attention to the structure of our thoughts and language in the Here-Now, we can shift to experiencing the Here-Now. Can it be that simple? We can recognize truth by its beauty and simplicity. We can recognize the power of the Self-Powerment Model by experiencing it.

When we live in the Here-Now, we are able to drop all human conditioning with its entrenched and limited thought patterns and start anew. What world can we create when we do this? A world of infinite possibilities.

We can choose to reexamine our values and refocus on what has real meaning for us in our lives. We can choose to take action to create personal, work, and world environments that reflect our higher vision of what can be so. To take the most effective action, we need to draw not only from our ever-expanding cognitive abilities but also from the wisdom that comes to us from direct experience in the Here-Now. Such fertile ground produces healthy and compassionate relationships with our environment, with other people and nations, but most importantly, with ourselves.

From Model to action—this is your choice.

Footnotes

1. Tolle, E. *The Power of Now*. Novato, Calif.: New World Library, 1999.
2. Demasio, A. *Self Comes to Mind: Constructing the Conscious Brain, Pantheon*. 2010.
3. Johnson, S. *Where Good Ideas Come From*. Riverhead Trade, 2011.
4. Bohm, D. *On Dialogue*. New York: Routledge, 1996.
5. Zukav, G. *The Seat of the Soul*. New York: Simon & Schuster, 1990.
6. Tolle, E. *The Power of Now*. Novato, Calif.: New World Library, 1999.
7. Lorde, A. *Sister Outsider*. Freedom, Calif.: The Crossing Press, 1984.
8. Russell, P. *Waking Up in Time*. Novato, Calif.: Origin Press Inc., 1998.
9. Cavafy, Constantine *Ithaca*
10. Zukav, G. *The Dancing Wu Li Masters*. New York: Morrow & Co., 1979.
11. Zukav, G. *The Seat of the Soul*. New York: Simon & Schuster, 1990.
12. McFarlane, T., Ed. *Einstein and Buddha: The Parallel Sayings*. Berkeley, Calif.: Ulysses Press, 2002.

13. Pritchett, P. *Carpe Monona*. Texas: Pritchett Rummler-Brache, 2000.
14. Pritchett, P. *Carpe Mariana*. Texas: Pritchett Rummler-Brache, 2000.
15. Keller, L. *Science, Observation, and Mystery*, Parabola, 25:2, May 2000.
16. Zukav, G. *The Dancing Wu Li Masters*. New York: Morrow & Co., 1979.
17. Wilber, K. *The Collected Works of Ken Wilber*. Boston: Shambhala, 1999.
18. Bohm, D. *On Dialogue*. New York: Routledge, 1996.
19. Krishnamurti, J. *Educating the Educator* (course). Parabola. 25:3, August 2000.
20. Russell, P. *Waking Up in Time*. Novato, Calif.: Origin Press Inc., 1998.
21. Bohm, D. *On Dialogue*. New York: Routledge, 1996.
22. Zohar, D. *The Quantum Self*. New York: William Morrow & Co., 1990.
23. Abram, D. *The Spell of the Sensuous*. New York: Random House, 1996.

Glossary of Terms

(Fayespeak)

Centered: Attention focused inside ourselves on our multisensory data.

Conditioning: Learned thought structures that take us away from I Am, the place of self-powerment.

Conjoined intelligence: The creation of a new form of intelligence that results from the joining of the intelligence of a group of individuals.

Direct experience: The quieting of thought to allow a full openness to experience.

Grounded: The state of being in the present moment.

Here-Now: The state of being in the present moment without attention to thought. Attention is focused internally on multi-sensory experience.

I Am: The way Here-Now is expressed in our language and the way we associate ourselves with time and space. The I Am defines us in time and space.

Intuition: The direct perception of the truth.

Negation: That which isn't.

Piggyback: The act of taking a feeling and moving it from the body on to a thought.

Self-Powerment: The state of being secure, being in control, and feeling adequate, resulting from using feelings to stay in the present moment and focused internally on the self's multisensory data.

Wisdom: Knowledge of what is true or right coupled with just judgment as to action, discernment, or insight.

Wobble: The state one is in when a life situation takes one out of the Here-Now.

Bibliography

Abram, D. *The Spell of the Sensuous*. New York: Random House, 1996.

Bohm, D. *On Dialogue*. New York: Routledge, 1996.

Capra, F. *The Web of Life*. New York: Random House, 1996.

Capra, F. *The Tao of Physics*, 4th ed. Boston: Shambala, 2000.

Cole, K. C. *First You Build a Cloud*. Orlando, Fla.: Harcourt Brace & Co. 1999.

DeMello, A. *Awareness*. New York: Doubleday, 1992.

Dossey, L. *Space, Time, and Medicine*. Boulder, Colo.: Shambala, 1982.

Edelman, G. and G. Tononi. *A Universe of Consciousness*. New York: Basic Books, 2000.

Elgin, D. *Awakening Earth*. New York: William Morrow & Co., 1993.

Houston, J. *The Hero and the Goddess*. New York: Random House, 1992.

Isaacson, W. *Steve Jobs*. New York: Simon and Schuster, 2011.

Keller, L. *Science, Observation, and Mystery*. Parabola. 25: 2, May 2000.

Krishnamurti, J. *Educating the Educator*. Parabola, 25: 3, August 2000.

Lorde, A. *Sister Outsider*. Calif.: The Crossing Press, 1984.

McFarlane, T. Ed. *Einstein & Buddha: The Parallel Sayings*. Calif.: Ulysses Press, 2002.

Pritchett, P. *Carpe Mariana*. Texas: Pritchett Rummer Brache, 2000.

Rickman, J. *General Selection from Works of Sigmund Freud*. New York: Doubleday & Co. Inc., 1957.

Russell, P. *Waking Up in Time*. Novato, Calif.: Origin Press Inc., 1998.

Thomas, L. *The Lives of a Cell*. New York: Penguin Books, 1978.

About the
Author

FAYE MANDELL has a Ph.D. in Counseling Psychology from Boston College. She travels extensively, leading workshops throughout the country. Her clients include several Fortune 500 companies. Dr. Mandell lives in Boca Raton, Florida.

How does it feel to be Alice in Wonderland? Where everything is not as it seems ... Going down the rabbit hole and discovering that what you knew to be real was only an illusion ... Being able to change shapes from big to small ... Being able to render time meaningless as we are "late for a very important date." Being able to change form ... from a flamingo to a crochet mallet ... And ... to return to "where everything is as it seems."

I feel a kindred spirit to Alice ... and so many other "characters" both real and created by extraordinary people ... I am clearly the "wicked queen" in *Snow White* ... I am Rizzo in the movie *Grease* ... I am Maria Tallchief ... I am a New England Patriots Fan ... I am a mama to the 3 most extraordinary children in the world ... I am a person of service ... I am a lover of wine, men, and song ... I am Sequoia, wise woman ...

I am the kid in the closet waiting for someone to come and get me ... I am an addict ... I am a teacher ... I am at the extremes of all things ... and totally in the middle ... I am Morpheus in *The Matrix* ... I am on the spirit tree in *Avatar* ... I am the white light people in Cocoon ...

The universe picked me at random to help transform our world ... My special friend Albert Einstein ... I have adopted relativity, and I hope that Albert Einstein is proud to share with me in executing on it.

Time and Space are our compass points ... My special friend, Steve Jobs, called it the reality distortion field. I have adopted it as my own, and I hope Steve is proud to share with me in executing on it. A reality distortion field is that place where you can see beyond the existence of forms created by people (culture). It is that place in which you see a "vast expanse in the moment" of time, space, scale, choice, trust, accountability ... This is the place that is free. It is available to everyone ... and the compass points ... the GPS is time and space ...

To be courageous ... My special friend, the Dalai Llama, says "The only thing needed to change the world is ... courage" I hope that the Dalai Llama is proud to share with me in executing on it ... to admit that what is so ... IS NOT!!!!

The miracle is here for everyone ... That is what is so exciting ... Welcome to my circle of friends ... Albert Einstein, Steve Jobs, The Dalai Llama, Eric Clapton,

Nelly, Maria Tallchief, are some of my circle of friends ...
Sooooooo many more.... . There is plenty of room for
you in here ... Who are you bringing??? Who are you???

Perspective, Gratitude, Balance, Focus ... these are
not concepts ... they are experiences that are FELT,
experienced ... That's what changes.... . You become
these ... They are not separate (in a different space that
you are) ... They are your manifesto ...

I stand in who I am despite the judgments of
others ...

So these are what I put my attention on.... . I am
engaged with the cosmos and atoms ... I love to work
out ... I love to make love ... I LOVE to laugh ... I love to
love ... In my work I speak to the authentic person, I see
The power in the structure ... I remove worry, anger, and
regret as drivers of behavior, I conjoin people to have the
whole be greater than the sum of the parts ... I revere
quality as well as quantity, I teach that measurement is
"in the eye of the beholder."

Learn how to get to the Present. Come be with me In
The Present ... Come down the rabbit hole.

You can also visit the website at:

www.being-present.com

http://www.youtube.com/watch?v=0dDOTPoTrRQ